AAT Advanced Diplo

Level 3

Indirect Tax

Finance Act 2019

Rosslyn Gabr

Fourth edition 2019

ISBN 9781 5097 8165 2

British Library Cataloguing-in-Publication Data

A catalogue record for this book is available from the British Library

Published by

BPP Learning Media Ltd,
BPP House, Aldine Place,
142-144 Uxbridge Road,
London W12 8AA

www.bpp.com/learningmedia

Printed in the United Kingdom

Your learning materials, published by BPP Learning Media Ltd, are printed on paper obtained from traceable sustainable sources.

Welcome to BPP Learning Media's AAT **Passcards for Indirect Tax FA 2019**.

- They **save you time**. Important topics are summarised for you.
- They incorporate **diagrams** to kick start your memory.
- They follow the overall **structure** of the BPP Course Book, but BPP Learning Media's AAT **Passcards** are not just a condensed book. Each card has been separately designed for clear presentation. Topics are self-contained and can be grasped visually.
- AAT **Passcards** are **just the right size** for pockets and bags where bought for studying on the move.
- AAT **Passcards focus on the assessment** you will be facing.
- AAT **Passcards focus on the essential points** that you need to know in the workplace, or when completing your computer based assessment.

Run through the complete set of **Passcards** as often as you can during your final revision period. The day before the assessment, try to go through the **Passcards** again! You will then be well on your way to completing the assessment successfully.

Good luck!

Page

The BPP **Question Bank** contains activities and practice assessments that provide invaluable practice in the skills you need to complete this unit successfully.

1–2: Introduction to VAT & VAT basics

Topic List

Introduction to VAT

Scope of VAT

Registration and deregistration

VAT is a tax with many detailed rules. The reference material provided throughout the assessment gives details of many of the VAT rules, however you must be confident in applying these rules to the tasks presented in the assessment.

In these chapters you need to understand the basic principles of the VAT system, how it operates, and the different types of supply.

You should also study the strict rules surrounding VAT registration, how to determine when a trader should register, why a trader might register voluntarily, and the circumstances when a trader may choose to deregister.

Value Added Tax (VAT)

- Indirect tax
- Normally borne by the final consumer
- Administered by HM Revenue & Customs (HMRC)
- Collected by VAT-registered traders in the course of their business

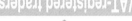

VAT-registered traders

- Charge OUTPUT tax on sales — Paid to HMRC
- Reclaim INPUT tax on expenses — Reclaimed from HMRC
- Input tax deducted from output tax
- Net payment/repayment submitted to HMRC
- VAT return completed — Usually every three months

VAT is normally borne by the final consumer.

Manufacturing process

Materials supplier
- Sells material for £1,000 plus VAT of £200

Manufacturer
- Buys material and sells goods on for £3,000 plus VAT of £600

Retailer
- Buys goods and sells on for £4,600 plus VAT of £920

Customer
- Buys goods for £4,600 plus VAT of £920

	VAT payments to HMRC
Keep £1,000 and pay over £200 to HMRC	£200 +
Keep £3,000 and pay over £400 to HMRC (£600 – £200)	£400 +
Keep £4,600 and pay over £320 to HMRC (£920 – £600)	£320 +
Pays nothing directly to HMRC but the whole £5,520 (£4,600 + £920) is paid to the shop	£0 = £920

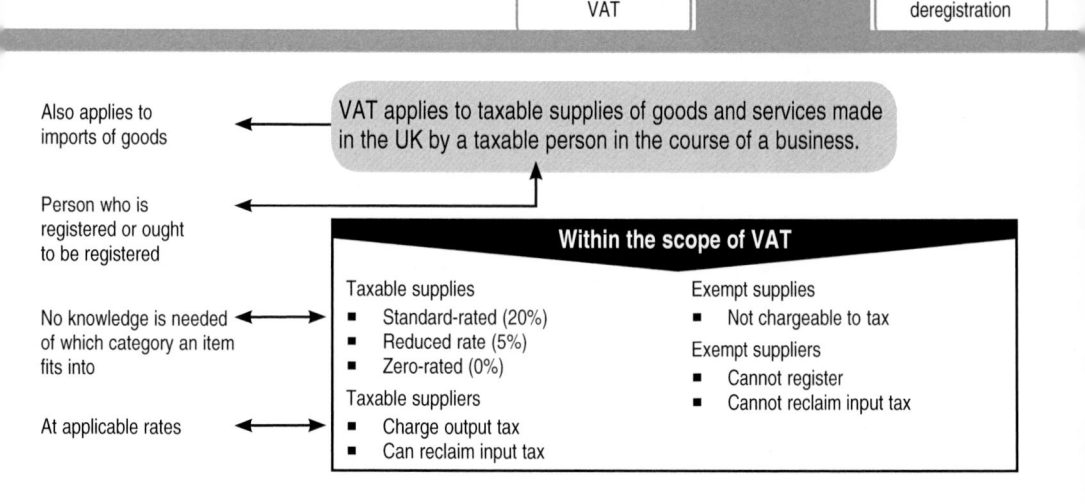

Also applies to imports of goods

VAT applies to taxable supplies of goods and services made in the UK by a taxable person in the course of a business.

Person who is registered or ought to be registered

Within the scope of VAT

No knowledge is needed of which category an item fits into

Taxable supplies
- Standard-rated (20%)
- Reduced rate (5%)
- Zero-rated (0%)

Taxable suppliers

At applicable rates
- Charge output tax
- Can reclaim input tax

Exempt supplies
- Not chargeable to tax

Exempt suppliers
- Cannot register
- Cannot reclaim input tax

Compulsory registration	Voluntary registration

Compulsory registration

Must register within 30 days if:

1 At the end of a month, the value of taxable supplies (excl. VAT) exceeds the registration limit in last 12 calendar months, or

Includes standard-rated, reduced rate and zero-rated.

Must register without delay if:

2 At any time, there are reasonable grounds for believing that the value of taxable supplies will exceed the registration limit in the next 30 days alone.

Voluntary registration

A trader can choose to be VAT-registered even though his supplies fall below the registration threshold.

Advantage

☑ Input VAT can be reclaimed

Disadvantages

☒ Administrative burden

☒ Possible penalties

☒ Non VAT-registered customers disadvantaged

The current examinable registration limit is £85,000 (FA19).

A trader making mainly zero-rated supplies can apply to HMRC to be exempt from registering.

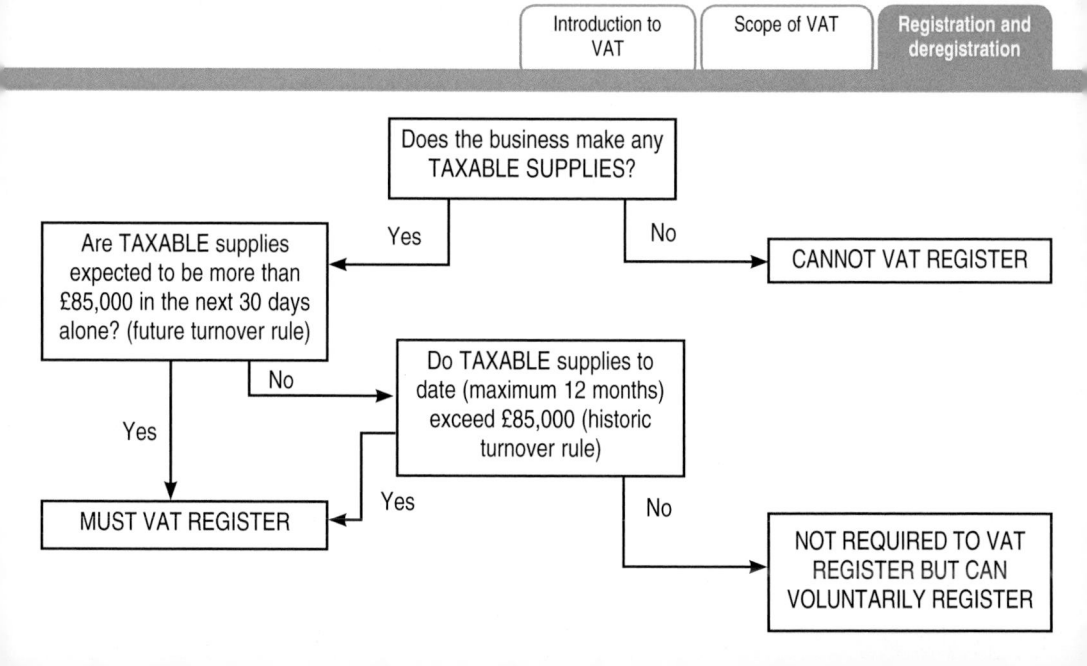

Voluntary deregistration

Suppliers can deregister voluntarily if the value of taxable supplies in the following 12-month period will not exceed £83,000 (FA19 limit).

Threshold exceeded temporarily

Traders can apply for exemption from registration if they can demonstrate that the threshold has been exceeded only temporarily.

Failure to register

Supplies made after the effective registration date are deemed to be VAT-inclusive. The trader must pay the appropriate VAT on these sales to HMRC. The trader can seek to recover this VAT from the customers.

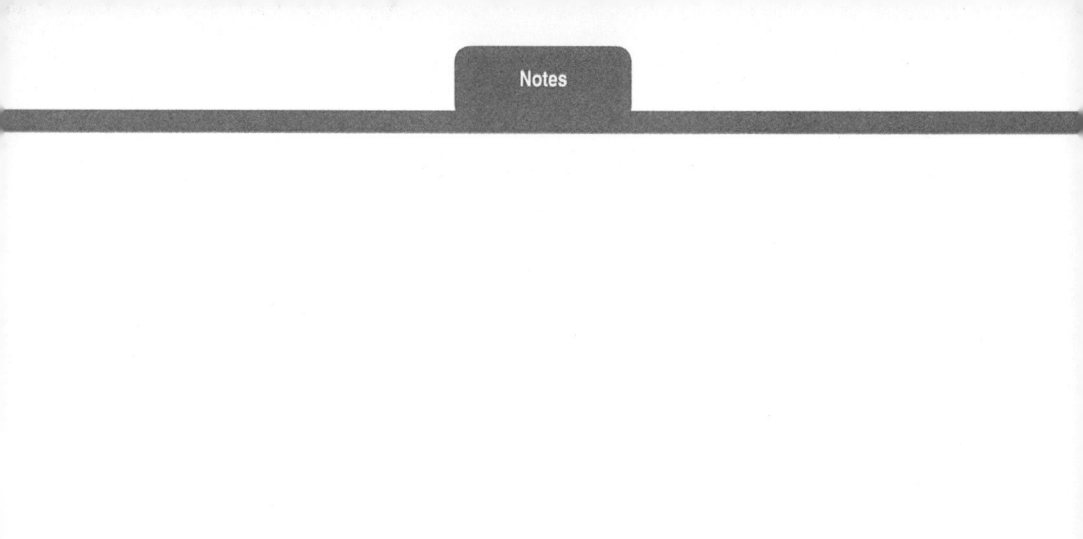

Notes

3: Inputs and outputs

Topic List

Calculation of VAT

Reclaiming input tax

Partial exemption

Overseas transactions

Within the VAT rules there are special rules for specific types of input and output.

Much of the detail of these rules can be found in the reference material provided throughout the live assessment, however you must be confident in how to apply the rules.

VAT on a standard rate supply is:

1   20% of the VAT-exclusive price

2   1/6 of the VAT-inclusive price

Valuation

The normal treatment for rounding is to round down to the nearest penny.

Business entertaining

- Input tax on business entertaining cannot be reclaimed. ← Can reclaim if entertaining overseas customers
- Input tax on entertaining staff can be reclaimed.

Cars & vans

- Input tax cannot be reclaimed on the purchase of a car. ← If there is any private use
- Input tax can be reclaimed on the purchase of a van.

Exceptions

Cars used:

- Exclusively for business purposes
- Within a taxi business
- For driving instruction
- Within a self-hire business

Fuel scale charge

Increase the amount payable to HMRC ↑

- Reclaim input tax on the purchase of all fuel ←
- Pay output tax if there is private use of fuel: quarterly fuel scale charge x 1/6

When input tax cannot be recovered, the cost to the business is the VAT-inclusive (gross) amount.

Capital items

Capital item	Input tax recoverable on purchase?	Charge output tax on sale?
Van	YES	YES
Most cars	NO	NO (exempt)

A business that makes some taxable and some exempt supplies is a partially exempt trader.

Apportion input tax between:

- Taxable supplies
- Exempt supplies

VAT attributable to taxable supplies

Input VAT relating wholly to taxable supplies is fully recoverable.

VAT attributable to exempt supplies

Input VAT relating wholly to exempt supplies may be recoverable, subject to the *de minimis* limits.

De minimis limit

All input VAT is recoverable if the total input VAT attributable to exempt supplies is below the *de minimis* limit.

Outside the EU

Exports of goods to outside the EU are zero-rated.

Imports of goods from outside the EU are subject to VAT at the same rate as on a purchase of same goods within the UK.

Output VAT is paid to HMRC at the port/airport, and input VAT is reclaimed on the VAT return (Box 4), giving a net effect of NIL.

Inside the EU

Despatches
When a taxable person supplies goods to a customer in another EU country, the supply is zero-rated if the customer is VAT registered and his registration number is shown on the invoice otherwise the supply will be charged as if a normal UK sale.

Acquisitions
When goods are brought into the UK from within the EU, the VAT registered customer has to charge himself VAT (at UK rates). The VAT due is shown on the next VAT return of the UK customer.

Output VAT is paid to HMRC on the VAT return (Box 2), and input VAT is reclaimed on the VAT return (Box 4), giving a net effect of NIL. No cash changes hands.

These rules are, as yet, still in place post EU referendum.

4: Accounting for VAT

Topic List

Keeping records

VAT invoices

Discounts

Tax point

Bad debt relief

VAT-registered traders must keep detailed records in order to determine the correct amounts to be included on the VAT return.

Detailed rules exist determining exactly what information must be shown on a valid VAT invoice. A list outlining which records need to be kept, and what should be included on an invoice is included in the detailed reference material available throughout the assessment.

This chapter also looks at the 'Tax point' of a transaction and how to reclaim the output VAT on an invoice that hasn't been paid.

VAT records must be kept for six years.

Records must be kept up-to-date and in a way in which allows:
- The calculations of VAT due
- Officers of HMRC to check the figures on VAT returns

Sources of information:
- Sales day book – invoices to credit customers
- Sales returns day book – credit notes to credit customers
- Cash receipts book – cash received
- Purchases day book – invoices from credit suppliers
- Purchases returns day book – credit notes from credit suppliers
- Cash payments book – payments made
- Petty cash records
- The journal – eg bad debts
- A VAT account

Traders must keep:

1 A summary of supplies made including:
- Standard-rate
- Reduced-rate
- Zero-rate
- Exempt

2 A summary of supplies received including:
- Standard-rate
- Reduced-rate
- Zero-rate
- Exempt

3 Details of trade overseas (EU and non EU)

4 Details of any non-standard adjustments made for VAT purposes

Invoices: required details

- Name, address and VAT no. of supplier
- Name and address of customer
- Invoice no., date of issue and tax point
- Total amount of VAT charged

For each different type of item:

- Description of goods or services supplied
- Quantity and unit price (excl. of VAT)
- Rate of VAT and VAT-exclusive total amount
- Rate of cash or settlement discount

Simplified (less detailed invoices)

May be issued where an invoice amount is no more than £250 (incl. VAT)

Credit notes issued to customers:

- Decreases output VAT
- Decreases amount payable to HMRC

Credit notes obtained from suppliers:

- Decreases input VAT
- Decreases amount reclaimable from HMRC

Pro forma invoice

- Cannot be used to reclaim input VAT
- Must be clearly marked 'THIS IS NOT A VAT INVOICE'

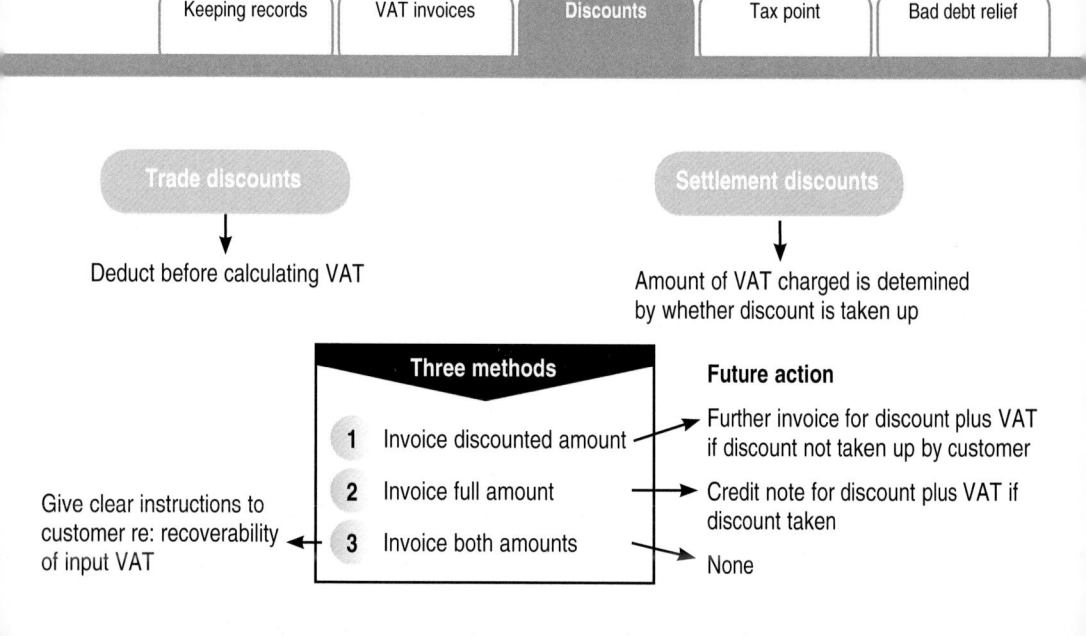

Each supply is treated as taking place on the **tax point.**

Basic tax point

- Goods: date on which goods removed/made available to customer
- Services: date service is completed

Actual tax point

Date invoice issued or payment made if **before** basic tax point.

Alternatively, if the earlier tax point is not used, the invoice date, if invoice issued within 14 days after basic tax point.

Deposits and advance payments

There may be two tax points when a deposit is paid – one for the deposit and another for the balance.

Pro forma invoice

Pro forma invoices have no impact for tax point. Wait for the real VAT invoice before determining tax point.

Tax point on the deposit is often the payment date as this usually occurs before delivery.

Bad debt relief

- Claim output VAT accounted for back from HMRC
- Bad debt must be more than six months overdue, and less than four years and six months old ■
- Debt must be written-off in business's accounts

Measured from when payment is due ■

Increases the INPUT VAT to be
reclaimed on VAT return (Box 4)

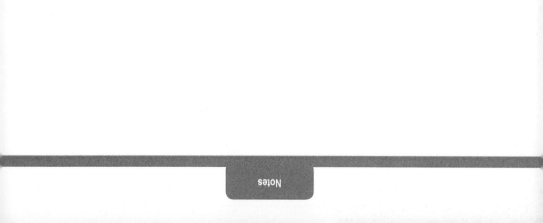

Notes

5: The VAT return

Topic List

VAT account

VAT return

Submitting the VAT return

In the assessment you will be required to complete a VAT return. Therefore it is essential that you spend time practising what goes in each box on the return.

Detailed reference material available throughout the assessment includes a section on 'completing the VAT return box by box'.

The VAT account provides a link between business records and the VAT return.

Input tax (VAT deductible) includes:

- VAT on credit purchases – from purchases day book
- VAT on cash purchases – from cash book & petty cash book
- Bad debt relief
- Error adjustments – under/(overstatement)
- VAT allowable from EU acquisitions
- (Deduction for credit notes from suppliers – from purchases returns day book)

Output tax (VAT payable) includes:

- VAT on credit sales – from sales day book
- VAT on cash sales – from cash book
- Fuel scale charge
- Error corrections – under/(overstatement)
- VAT due on EU acquisitions
- (Deduction for credit notes to customers – from sales returns day book)

Note. If the VAT account is presented as a traditional double entry account, the credit notes will be shown on opposite sides to the purchases/sales to which they relate as they are reducing either the input or output VAT accordingly.

- The balance of the VAT account must agree with the figure on the VAT return.
- When payment is made to HMRC, this will clear the VAT account ready for the next VAT accounting period.

VAT due in this period on sales and other outputs	Box 1	
VAT due in this period on acquisitions from other EC Member States	Box 2	
Total VAT due (the sum of boxes 1 and 2)	Box 3	
VAT reclaimed in this period on purchases and other inputs, including acquisitions from EC	Box 4	
Net VAT to be paid to HM Revenue & Customs or reclaimed by you (Difference between boxes 3 and 4)	Box 5	
Total value of sales and all other outputs excluding any VAT. Include your box 8 figure	Box 6	
		Whole pounds only
Total value of purchases and all other inputs excluding any VAT. Include your box 9 figure	Box 7	
		Whole pounds only
Total value of all supplies of goods and related costs, excluding any VAT, to other EC Member States	Box 8	
		Whole pounds only
Total value of all acquisitions of goods and related costs, excluding any VAT, from other EC Members States	Box 9	
		Whole pounds only

The VAT return must be completed and submitted to arrive no later than DUE DATE.

A trader accounts for VAT for each **VAT period**. Periods are normally three months long, but they may last for 12 months (see 'Annual accounting'). A VAT return is completed for each period.

Box 1 includes fuel scale charges.

Box 4 includes bad debt relief.

Boxes on a VAT return

Box 1: VAT due on sales/other outputs

Box 2: VAT due on EU acquisitions

Box 3: Total of Boxes 1 and 2

Box 4: Input VAT on purchases/other inputs

Box 5: Net VAT due/reclaimable

Box 6: Total of sales/other outputs excl. VAT

Box 7: Total of purchases/other inputs excl. VAT

Box 8: Total sales etc to EU members

Box 9: Total purchases etc from EU members

Figures shown in pounds and pence.

Figures in whole pounds.

VAT return and payment due dates

Nearly all traders are required to file VAT returns online and pay electronically using the Making Tax Digital service.

Online return

Return due date

- One month and seven calendar days following the end of the return period

Payment due date

- Electronic payment – Online return date
- Direct debit – Online return date plus extra three bank working days

---

5: The VAT return

Notes

6: VAT schemes for small businesses

Topic List

Cash accounting

Annual accounting

Flat rate scheme

Several schemes exist to help reduce the burden of VAT administration for small businesses. You should ensure that you know the benefits and implications of each scheme.

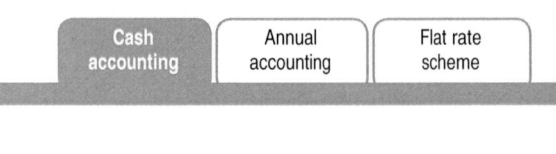

Cash accounting scheme

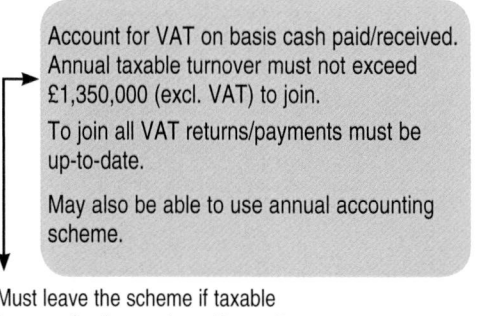

Account for VAT on basis cash paid/received. Annual taxable turnover must not exceed £1,350,000 (excl. VAT) to join.

To join all VAT returns/payments must be up-to-date.

May also be able to use annual accounting scheme.

Must leave the scheme if taxable turnover for the previous 12 months exceeds £1,600,000 (excl. VAT)

Advantages
☑ Useful where long period of credit given to customers
☑ Automatic bad debt relief

As OUTPUT VAT will never be paid over to HMRC on bad debts

As OUTPUT VAT will be paid over to HMRC later

Disadvantage
☒ Less beneficial where long periods of credit received from suppliers

Annual accounting scheme

- Annual taxable turnover must not exceed £1,350,000 (excl. VAT) to join
- Annual VAT return due two months after the year end
- Payments of VAT needed during year

Must leave the scheme if taxable turnover for the previous 12 months exceeds £1,600,000 (excl. VAT)

End of months 4–12 pay 1/10 of previous year's liability. Pay the balance of VAT with the return

- Must be up to date with all VAT returns/payments
- Can also use cash a/c scheme **or** flat rate scheme

Advantages

- ☑ Only one return each year
- ☑ Payments spread evenly throughout most of the year

Disadvantages

- ☒ Monitor supplies to ensure the turnover limit is not exceeded.
- ☒ Payments based on previous year's turnover may not reflect current year's activities.

Flat rate scheme

Business can calculate VAT due by applying a flat rate percentage to VAT-inclusive taxable turnover.

The business must have annual taxable turnover (excl. VAT) of no more than £150,000 to join.

May also be able to use annual accounting scheme.

Must leave the scheme if TOTAL turnover exceeds £230,000 (incl. VAT)

Flat rate percentage usually depends on industry, but always 16.5% for limited cost traders

Advantages

- ☑ Simplifies administration – do not need to deal with VAT on purchase invoices
- ☑ Can lead to less VAT payable
- ☑ Discount of 1% given in first year of registration

Disadvantages

- ☒ Cannot reclaim VAT on purchases and expenses (except fixed assets over £2,000 incl VAT)
- ☒ Flat rate applied to all turnover including zero-rated and exempt supplies
- ☒ More VAT may be payable

7: Administration

Topic List

Errors

Penalties

Changes in VAT legislation

Contact with HMRC

Ethics

In the event of discovering an error on a VAT return, it is sensible to rectify this as soon as possible to mitigate any possible penalties.

In each assessment you will be required to complete a letter or email on VAT matters. For example you may be asked to communicate payment information including amounts and time limits. It is essential that you practise this skill.

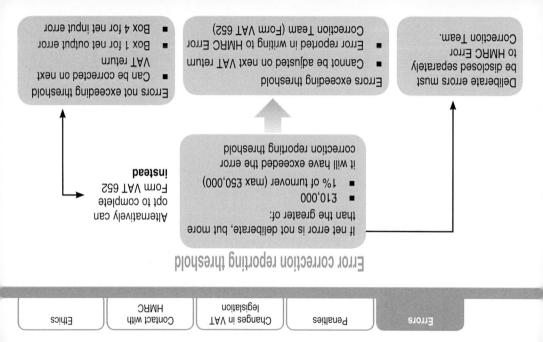

Error correction reporting threshold

If net error is not deliberate, but more than the greater of:
- £10,000
- 1 % of turnover (max £50,000)

it will have exceeded the error correction reporting threshold

Errors not exceeding threshold
- Can be corrected on next VAT return
  - Box 1 for net output error
  - Box 4 for net input error

Alternatively can opt to complete Form VAT 652 instead

Errors exceeding threshold
- Cannot be adjusted on next VAT return
- Error reported in writing to HMRC Error Correction Team (Form VAT 652)

Deliberate errors must be disclosed separately to HMRC Error Correction Team.

Late returns/payments

- Issued with a surcharge liability notice (SLN)
- SLN last 12 months
- Payment default in period leads to surcharge

Careless and deliberate errors

- These will be liable for a penalty, whether adjusted on next return or reported separately.

Failure to keep records

- Records should be kept for six years.
- Penalty could be imposed.

Assessments

- If a VAT return is not submitted, HMRC can raise an assessment on what they believe is owed.
- If business fails to notify within 30 days that this amount is too low, they may be liable for a penalty.

Inaccurate return

- Penalty can be reduced if tell HMRC ASAP.

Failure to register

- A penalty can be imposed for failure to register by proper date.

Fraudulent evasion of VAT

- Falsely reclaiming input VAT/understating output VAT

- Falsely obtaining bad debt relief

- Falsely obtaining a repayment

- Tax **avoidance** is legal
- Tax **evasion** is a criminal offence

Penalties

- Minor cases of evasion will be settled with penalties

- More extreme cases might result in fines and/or imprisonment

HMRC

Notifies changes via:

- Bulletins
- Notices
- Website

Effect on cash flow

Communicate VAT payment amounts and due dates internally

Impact on systems and customers

Computerised systems may need adaptation to accommodate changes in legislation. Support may be needed from software house.

Customers may need to be informed of significant changes that affect them.

Sales/marketing/accounts staff should also all be informed of changes that affect them.

→ Eg change in VAT rate

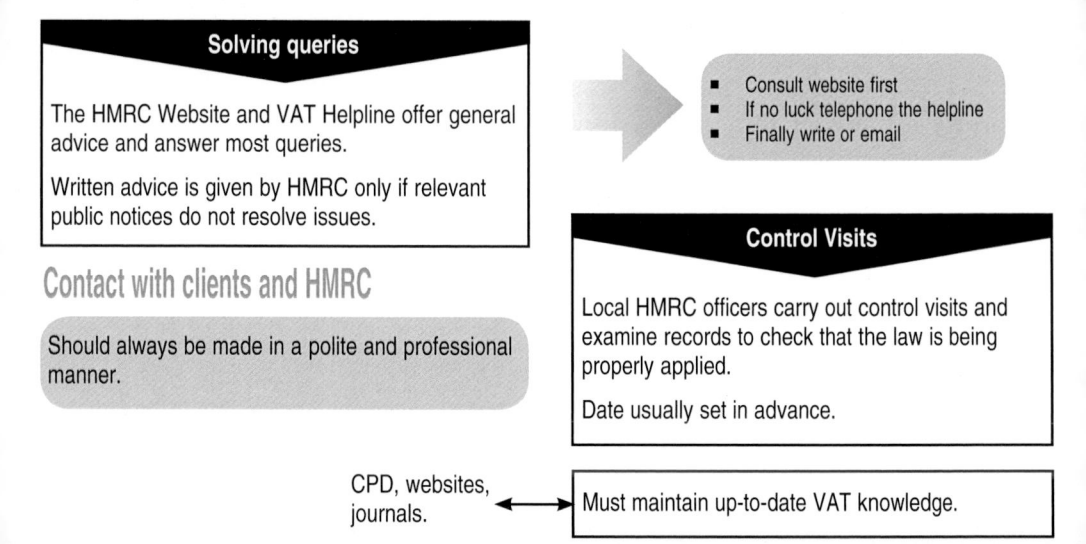

| Errors | Penalties | Changes in VAT legislation | **Contact with HMRC** | Ethics |

Solving queries

The HMRC Website and VAT Helpline offer general advice and answer most queries.

Written advice is given by HMRC only if relevant public notices do not resolve issues.

- Consult website first
- If no luck telephone the helpline
- Finally write or email

Contact with clients and HMRC

Should always be made in a polite and professional manner.

Control Visits

Local HMRC officers carry out control visits and examine records to check that the law is being properly applied.

Date usually set in advance.

CPD, websites, journals. ←→ Must maintain up-to-date VAT knowledge.

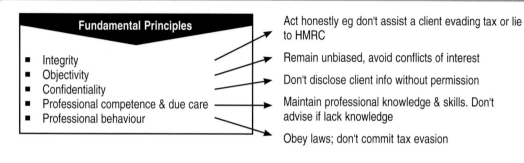

Fundamental Principles

- Integrity
- Objectivity
- Confidentiality
- Professional competence & due care
- Professional behaviour

Act honestly eg don't assist a client evading tax or lie to HMRC

Remain unbiased, avoid conflicts of interest

Don't disclose client info without permission

Maintain professional knowledge & skills. Don't advise if lack knowledge

Obey laws; don't commit tax evasion

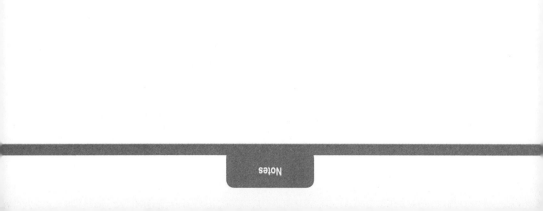
Notes

Notes

Notes